THE SPACE RACE

PROJECT APOLLO

BY JOHN HAMILTON

Abdo & Daughters
An imprint of Abdo Publishing | abdobooks.com

abdobooks.com

Published by Abdo Publishing, a division of ABDO, PO Box 398166, Minneapolis, Minnesota 55439. Copyright © 2019 by Abdo Consulting Group, Inc. International copyrights reserved in all countries. No part of this book may be reproduced in any form without written permission from the publisher. Abdo & Daughters™ is a trademark and logo of Abdo Publishing.

Printed in the United States of America, North Mankato, Minnesota.
012019
012019

THIS BOOK CONTAINS RECYCLED MATERIALS

Editor: Sue Hamilton
Copy Editor: Bridget O'Brien
Graphic Design: John Hamilton
Cover Design: Candice Keimig and Pakou Moua
Cover Photo: NASA
Interior Images: All images NASA, except Alamy-pgs 12-13 (top); Getty-pg 17; John Hamilton-pg 9 (bottom diagram); Science Source-pg 8 (left); Shutterstock-pg 6.

Library of Congress Control Number: 2018950013
Publisher's Cataloging-in-Publication Data
Names: Hamilton, John, author.
Title: Project Apollo / by John Hamilton.
Description: Minneapolis, Minnesota : Abdo Publishing, 2019 | Series: The space race | Includes online resources and index.
Identifiers: ISBN 9781532118319 (lib. bdg.) | ISBN 9781532171567 (ebook)
Subjects: LCSH: Project Apollo (U.S.)--Juvenile literature. | Manned space flight--History--Juvenile literature. | Space flight--History--Juvenile literature. | Space race--Juvenile literature.
Classification: DDC 629.454--dc23

CONTENTS

The First Footsteps on the Moon........................ 4
Moon Probes 6
Monster Rockets 8
The Apollo Spacecraft 10
A Trip to the Moon 12
Apollo 1 Tragedy 14
Soyez 1 16
Apollo 7 18
Apollo 8 20
Apollo 9 24
Apollo 10 25
Apollo 11 26
Apollo 12 32
Apollo 13 34
Apollo 14 36
Apollo 15 38
Apollo 16 40
Apollo 17 42
Timeline 44
Glossary 46
Online Resources 47
Index 48

THE FIRST FOOTSTEPS ON THE MOON

On July 20, 1969, American astronauts Neil Armstrong and Buzz Aldrin became the first humans to land on the Moon. It was the climax of the Space Race, a fierce competition between the United States and the Soviet Union (much of which is today's Russia).

Project Apollo built on the successes of the Mercury and Gemini space programs. The Apollo program spanned more than a decade and was overseen by three presidents. The cost to the nation was more than $25 billion. Tragically, three astronauts lost their lives in a launchpad fire in 1967.

Despite all the hardships, landing astronauts on the Moon gave America great prestige in the eyes of the world. Project Apollo advanced science and gave us new technology. It also fulfilled a dream as old as humanity: to send people to the Moon and bring them safely back to Earth.

EXPLORING ANOTHER WORLD

A close-up view of astronaut Buzz Aldrin's bootprint in the lunar soil, taken during the Apollo 11 crew's landing and exploration of the Moon in 1969.

5

MOON PROBES

Apollo 11 landed on the Moon in 1969, but the National Aeronautics and Space Administration (NASA) tried for many years beforehand to learn as much as possible about our lunar neighbor. Even by the late 1950s, scientists knew surprisingly little about the Moon. We only knew there was no air to breathe, and no water. There were no detailed maps, and the far side of the Moon (the side that always faces away from Earth) had never been seen by any satellite. The surface was still a mystery.

Along with NASA, the Soviet Union's space program was also hard at work trying to find out about the Moon. The Soviets and Americans were locked in the Space Race. The country that had the most information about the Moon would have a big advantage when it came time to land a manned spacecraft on the lunar surface.

Between 1958 and 1969, the Soviet Union and the United States sent dozens of probes and landers to Earth's natural satellite. Most crashed or missed the Moon completely. On September 13, 1959, the Soviet Union's Luna 2 probe crashed on the surface, becoming the first human-made object to reach the Moon.

LUNA 2

The Soviet Union's Luna 2 probe (museum copy above) became the first human-made object to reach the Moon. It crashed on the surface.

The Soviets bragged that once again, their space program was superior to the Americans'. The closest NASA had gotten by this time was a flyby of the Pioneer 4 space probe, which came within 37,282 miles (60,000 km) of the Moon. Just a few weeks after Luna 2, the Soviet Union's Luna 3 probe took the first pictures of the far side of the Moon. On February 3, 1966, the Soviet's Luna 9 became the first probe to land softly on the Moon and send back pictures. Luna 9 proved that a lander would not sink into the soft lunar soil.

Despite the early Soviet successes, the United States kept trying. In 1964 and 1965, the Ranger 7, 8, and 9 probes took detailed photos of the Moon before crashing into the surface. Images were radioed back to Earth before they crashed. Maps made from the photos helped pick the sites for the later manned Apollo missions.

On June 2, 1966, NASA's Surveyor 1 made a soft landing on the Moon. It was the first of several American Surveyor landers. They took pictures and gathered information about the lunar surface, and even took soil samples.

SURVEYOR 1

NASA's Surveyor 1 landed on the Moon on June 2, 1966. The spacecraft transmitted data and photos from shortly after touchdown until July 14, 1966.

ESCAPE ROCKET

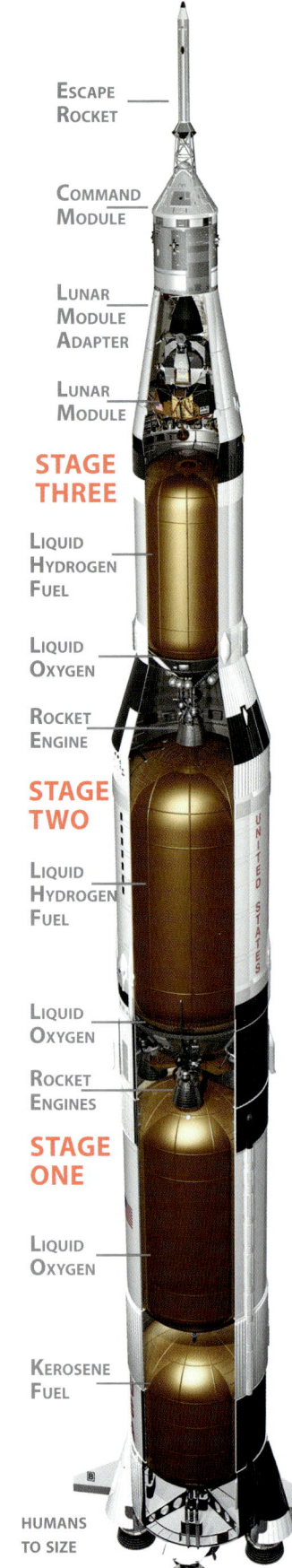

COMMAND MODULE

LUNAR MODULE ADAPTER

LUNAR MODULE

STAGE THREE

LIQUID HYDROGEN FUEL

LIQUID OXYGEN

ROCKET ENGINE

STAGE TWO

LIQUID HYDROGEN FUEL

LIQUID OXYGEN

ROCKET ENGINES

STAGE ONE

LIQUID OXYGEN

KEROSENE FUEL

HUMANS TO SIZE

MONSTER ROCKETS

Wernher von Braun stands near Saturn V rocket engines.

The Saturn V ("Saturn five") rockets used for the Apollo missions to the Moon were the biggest, most powerful rockets ever made. Sometimes nicknamed "monster rockets," they were designed by chief rocket engineer Wernher von Braun. He was a German-born scientist who worked for the United States after World War II. Von Braun and his team took six years to develop the complicated Saturn V rocket.

The three-stage Saturn V towered 363 feet (111 m) tall, nearly 60 feet (18 m) taller than the Statue of Liberty on its pedestal. It weighed 6.2 million pounds (2.8 million kg) fully fueled. The first stage produced 7.6 million pounds (3.4 million kg) of thrust during a two-minute burn. That's enough to launch the weight of 10 school busses into orbit. The five massive engines together gulped up to 20 tons (18 metric tons) of liquid fuel per second. The Saturn V had more than enough power to send three astronauts and their heavy spacecraft to the Moon.

While the Americans worked on the Saturn V, the Soviet Union was busy building a monster rocket of its own. It was called the N-1. Like the Saturn V, the N-1 was a three-stage rocket. It was the brainchild of the Soviet's chief rocket designer, Sergei Korolev. The N-1 was slightly shorter than the Saturn V, but its cluster of engines could produce more thrust. Sadly for the Soviets, each of the four unmanned N-1 launch attempts failed when the rockets either burst into flames or exploded. The N-1 failures set back the Soviet Moon program many years.

SOVIET N-1 ROCKET

The Soviet Union's space program developed a three-stage N-1 rocket similar to the American Saturn V.

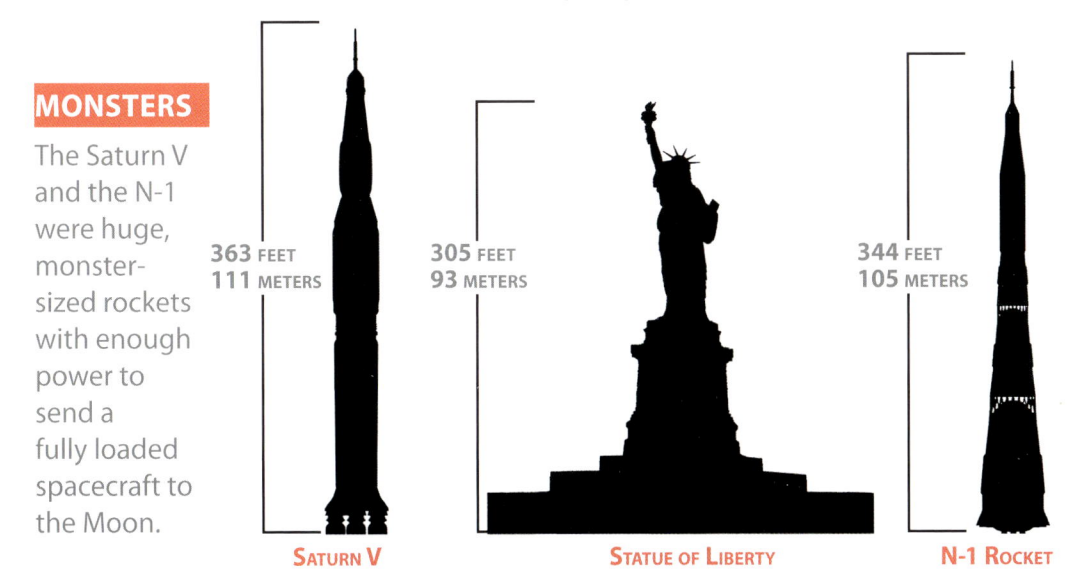

MONSTERS

The Saturn V and the N-1 were huge, monster-sized rockets with enough power to send a fully loaded spacecraft to the Moon.

363 FEET
111 METERS

305 FEET
93 METERS

344 FEET
105 METERS

SATURN V

STATUE OF LIBERTY

N-1 ROCKET

9

THE APOLLO SPACECRAFT

American astronauts traveled to the Moon in a spacecraft that was made up of three main parts, or modules. The part where the astronauts spent most of their time was called the command module. This conically shaped capsule was larger than the earlier Mercury or Gemini spacecraft. Three astronauts had room enough to move around and stretch when their seats were folded up. There was about the same amount of room inside as a large car.

The command module was covered with a heat shield that was thickest at the bottom. This protected the crew during the tremendous heat of reentry through Earth's atmosphere. Three large parachutes opened at the top just before splashing down in the ocean to cushion the impact.

Engine

Command Module

Service Module

Lunar Module

COMMAND MODULE
Height: 10 feet, 7 inches (3.2 m)
Diameter (base): 12 feet, 10 inches (3.9 m)
Weight: 13,000 pounds (5,897 kg)

SERVICE MODULE
Height: 24 feet, 7 inches (7.5 m)
Diameter: 12 feet, 10 inches (3.9 m)
Weight: 54,000 pounds (24,494 kg)

Attached to the rear of the command module was the cylinder-shaped service module. It held fuel for the voyage, fuel cells that made electricity, plus many scientific instruments. At the rear was the spacecraft's main rocket engine. The service module was separated from the command module just before reentry.

The lunar module was the part of the spacecraft that landed on the Moon. It had four legs that extended outward, with large pads on the end to keep the spacecraft from sinking into the lunar dust. The lunar module had two parts. When the Moon exploration was finished, only the top part returned to dock with the orbiting command module.

The lunar module was small inside, with just enough room for two people. It was a base for the astronauts during their exploration of the Moon. It had enough oxygen and other supplies for about a three-day mission on the surface.

LUNAR MODULE
Height: 22 feet, 11 inches (7 m)
Diameter: 31 feet (9.4 m)
Weight: 32,500 pounds (14,742 kg)

A TRIP TO THE MOON

When planning how to send astronauts to the Moon, NASA decided on a "lunar orbit rendezvous" type of flight. Instead of sending one gigantic rocket to land on the Moon and then travel back to Earth, the Apollo spacecraft was modular. Each part had a different job. Only the small lunar module landed on the surface. That meant not as much fuel needed to be carried all the way from Earth. Docking and undocking, however, could be dangerous. NASA decided it was worth the risk in order to avoid designing and building a larger rocket than necessary.

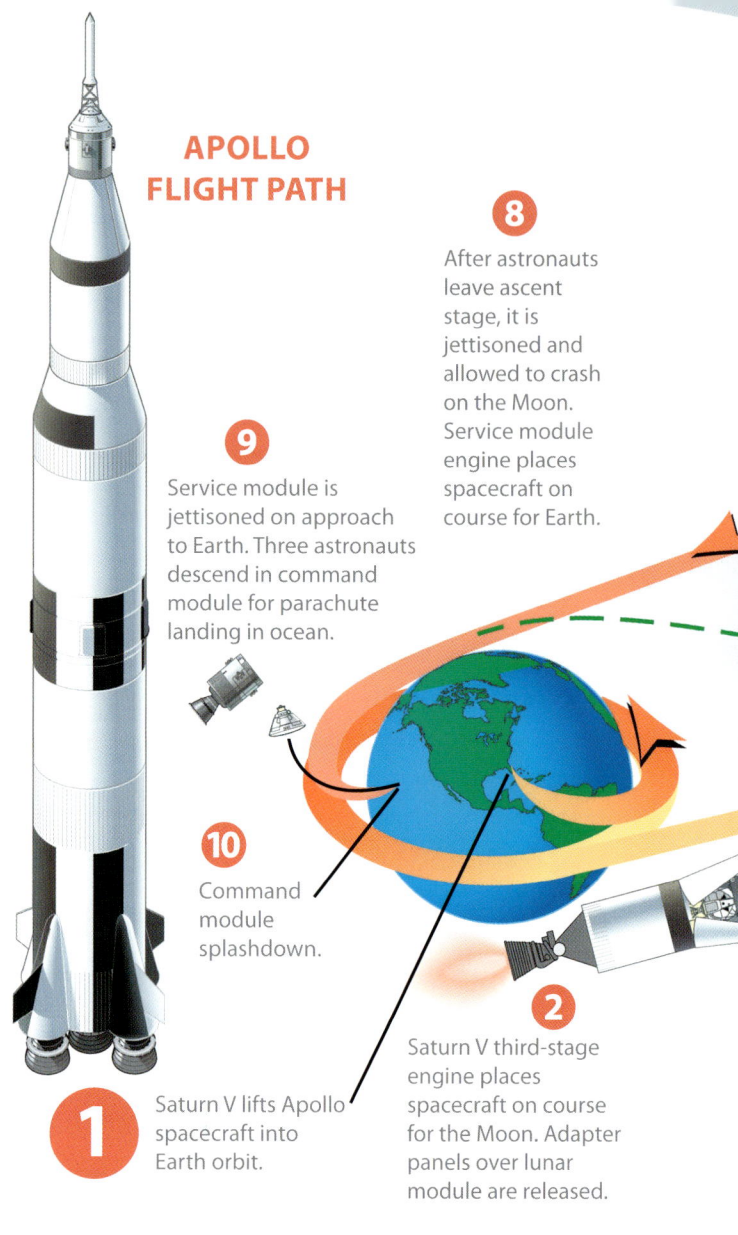

APOLLO FLIGHT PATH

8 After astronauts leave ascent stage, it is jettisoned and allowed to crash on the Moon. Service module engine places spacecraft on course for Earth.

9 Service module is jettisoned on approach to Earth. Three astronauts descend in command module for parachute landing in ocean.

10 Command module splashdown.

1 Saturn V lifts Apollo spacecraft into Earth orbit.

2 Saturn V third-stage engine places spacecraft on course for the Moon. Adapter panels over lunar module are released.

APOLLO MISSIONS

MANNED APOLLO SPACEFLIGHTS: 11

FIRST MANNED APOLLO FLIGHT: Apollo 7 (1968)

FIRST MOON LANDING: Apollo 11 (1969)

LAST MOON LANDING: Apollo 17 (1972)

TOTAL NUMBER OF ASTRONAUTS WHO WALKED ON THE MOON: 12

6 Lunar module ascent stage lifts off from lunar surface, leaving descent stage on the Moon.

7 Ascent stage achieves lunar orbit and docks with command and service modules.

Position of Moon at departure.

5 Lunar module, carrying two astronauts, separates and descends to the Moon's surface, while command and service modules, carrying one astronaut, remain in lunar orbit.

Position of Moon at lunar orbit insertion.

4 On the far side of the Moon, beyond radio communication, service module engine slows spacecraft to achieve lunar orbit.

3 Command and service modules separate from Saturn V third stage, turn end over end, and dock with lunar module. Saturn V third stage is jettisoned.

Free-return trajectory to be used in an emergency.

Position of Moon at launch.

MISSION CONTROL

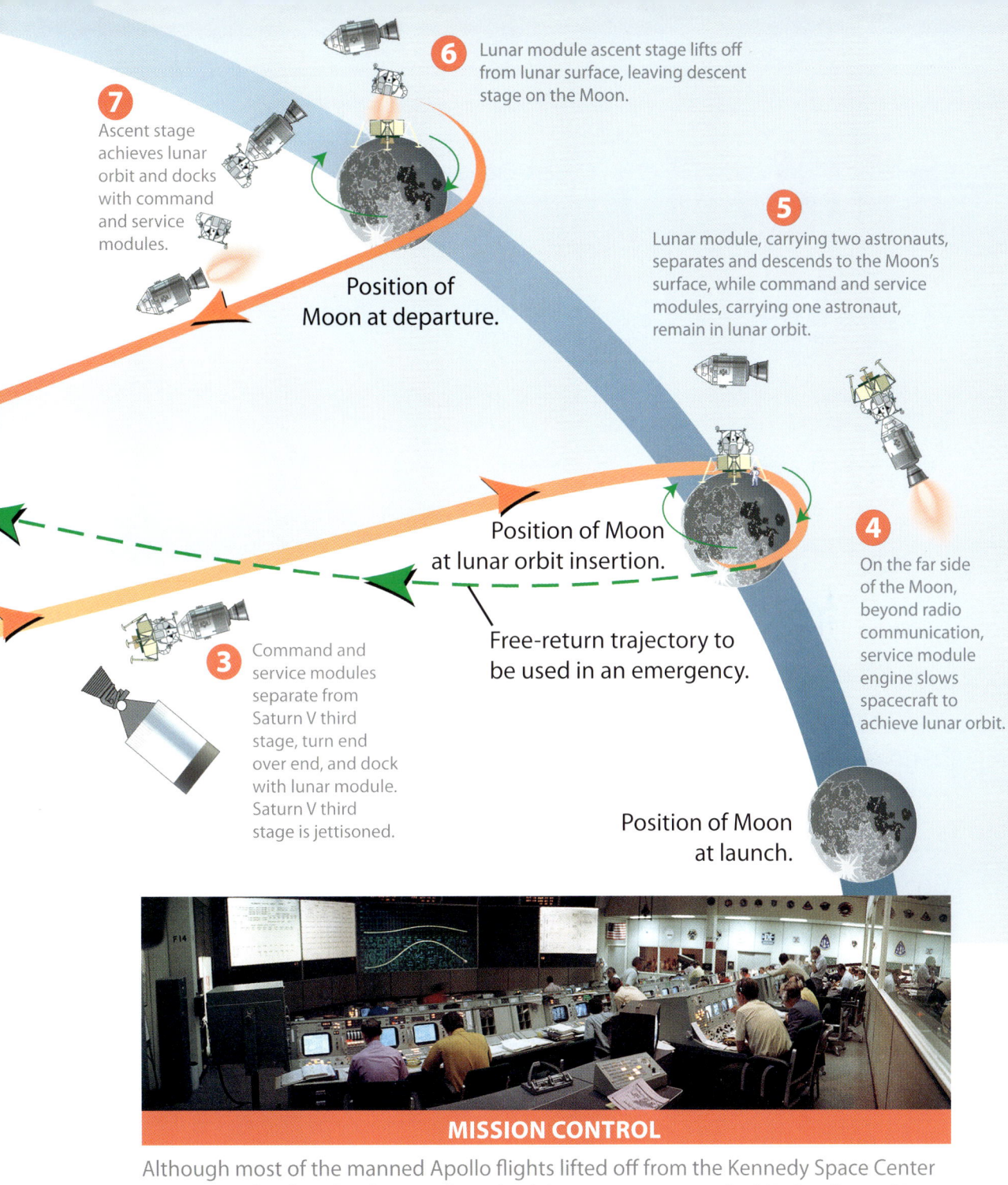

Although most of the manned Apollo flights lifted off from the Kennedy Space Center on Merritt Island in Florida, once launched they were overseen by Mission Control in Houston, Texas. Housed in Building 30 of today's Johnson Space Center, Mission Control was the workplace for dozens of flight controllers, computer technicians, and scientists during the Apollo missions. Apollo spacecraft were constantly tracked and monitored, and when trouble arose, it was up to Mission Control to help find solutions.

13

APOLLO 1 TRAGEDY

MISSION: Apollo 1
ROCKET: Saturn 1B
ACCIDENT DATE: January 27, 1967
ASTRONAUTS: Gus Grissom, Ed White, Roger Chaffee

February 21, 1967, was supposed to be the date of the first Apollo mission. Sadly, Apollo 1 ended before it even got off the ground. During a preflight test on January 27, a spark ignited the pure-oxygen atmosphere inside the command module. A flash fire raged inside the enclosed capsule. Astronauts Virgil "Gus" Grissom, Edward "Ed" White, and Roger Chaffee were killed within seconds.

Gus Grissom had flown on two previous space missions, one Mercury and one Gemini. He became the second American astronaut to go in space in 1961 in his Mercury *Liberty Bell 7* spacecraft. Like Grissom, astronaut Ed White also was a veteran of the Gemini program. He became the first American spacewalker during the Gemini 4 mission in 1965. Astronaut Roger Chaffee was a decorated U.S. Navy pilot. Apollo 1 would have been his first trip to space.

After the Apollo 1 launchpad tragedy, manned flights were suspended for almost two years. The fire resulted in a safer redesign of the command module, plus better safety and testing procedures.

LOST LIVES HELP FUTURE ASTRONAUTS

The burned command module was taken apart and studied to create a safer capsule for future missions. It was a tragic reminder of the dangers of spaceflight.

Apollo 1 astronauts Gus Grissom (left), Ed White (center), and Roger Chaffee (right) died when a fire erupted during a training exercise on the launchpad.

SOYEZ 1

As NASA mourned the loss of its three astronauts in the Apollo 1 fire, the Soviet Union found itself with a disaster of its own. By 1967, the Soviets had developed a new generation of spacecraft called Soyuz. It could change the direction of its orbit and dock with other spacecraft, like NASA's Gemini. However, Soyuz was also designed to go all the way to the Moon.

Vladimir Komarov

Soyez 1

Unmanned Soyuz test launches had uncovered many problems. The system wasn't fully ready. However, when the Apollo 1 disaster struck, Soviet leader Leonid Brezhnev saw a chance for his space program to shine.

The Soviets planned to launch a Soyuz spacecraft into orbit with a single cosmonaut aboard. A day later, three more cosmonauts would launch in a second Soyuz. After a rendezvous and docking in space, two of the cosmonauts would switch spacecraft. Brezhnev was sure the complicated and dangerous mission would show the world the superiority of the Communist system. Soviet spacecraft engineers warned their leaders that Soyuz wasn't ready, but their concerns were ignored.

The cosmonaut chosen to fly Soyuz 1 was Vladimir Komarov. He lifted off from the Soviet Baikonur Cosmodrome space center in Kazakhstan on April 23, 1967. Komarov's problems began soon after launch. One of Soyuz 1's solar panels did not unfold, and the spacecraft's flight system was unstable.

The next day, thunderstorms prevented Soyuz 2 from lifting off. There would be no rendezvous. Meanwhile, high above Earth, Komarov was having more trouble with Soyuz 1. Finally, the mission was aborted, and he was ordered to begin reentry after a little more than a day in orbit.

Cosmonaut Vladimir Komarov trains for his Soyuz 1 flight in 1967.

As Komarov plummeted through the atmosphere, he could barely control Soyuz 1. Then, the main parachute failed to open. Horrified onlookers watched as the spacecraft slammed into the ground at nearly 400 miles per hour (644 km/hr) and burst into flames. Komarov died instantly.

Cosmonauts didn't fly in space again until 18 months after the Soyuz 1 tragedy. The Soyuz capsule was redesigned and made safer (although three more cosmonauts died in the Soyuz 11 accident in 1971). But with such a long delay, the Soviet Union fell further behind the Americans in the race to the Moon.

APOLLO 7

MISSION: Apollo 7
ROCKET: Saturn 1B
DATE: October 11-22, 1968
ASTRONAUTS: Wally Schirra, Walt Cunningham, Donn Eisele

On October 11, 1968, Apollo 7 lifted off from Cape Canaveral, Florida, rising into space atop a pillar of orange flame. Astronauts Wally Schirra, Walt Cunningham, and Donn Eisele were flying inside a newly redesigned Apollo command module. Boosting them into space was a Saturn 1B rocket, a smaller two-stage version of the Saturn V. The larger rocket wasn't needed because the lunar module was left behind. Apollo 7's mission was to test the command and service modules.

Previous unmanned missions included Apollo 4, 5, and 6. (There was no Apollo 2 or 3.) The test flights were all successes, except for an engine failure on Apollo 6. Hopes were high for the first Apollo mission with a crew aboard.

APOLLO 7

The crew of the first manned Apollo space mission were, from left to right: Donn Eisele, command module pilot; Wally Schirra, commander; and Walt Cunningham, lunar module pilot.

Apollo 7 lifts off.

As Apollo 7 rose higher into the sky, Schirra radioed to Mission Control in Houston, Texas, "She's riding like a dream." When they were safely in orbit around Earth, the crew tested the command module's flight systems, including rendezvous and docking. They also performed science experiments, and broadcast live television images to Earth.

The crew was happy with the size of the new capsule. The earlier Mercury and Gemini cabins were very cramped. Inside the Apollo spacecraft, the astronauts could unstrap themselves and float around in the cabin. There was even a rest area beneath the seats for privacy.

After a successful mission, Apollo 7 splashed down in the Atlantic Ocean on October 22, 1968. They had flown for almost 11 days in orbit, which would have been enough time to get to the Moon and back.

AHHH-CHOO!

The only real problem on the Apollo 7 mission was a terrible cold picked up by Wally Schirra, which he passed on to the other two astronauts. In the weightlessness of space, mucus painfully fills the nasal passages and does not drain from the nose, like on Earth. The only thing the astronauts could do was blow their noses hard, which hurt their eardrums. Aspirin and decongestants helped with the pain, but the astronauts became grouchy with each other. They also ignored some orders from Mission Control, which got them in trouble after they landed.

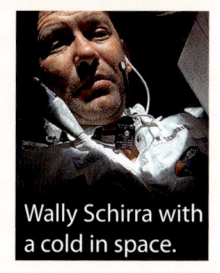

Wally Schirra with a cold in space.

APOLLO 8

After the success of Apollo 7, NASA had a bold plan for its second manned Apollo mission. The lunar module was not yet ready to land on the Moon. However, it appeared that the Soviet Union was preparing to soon send a spacecraft into lunar orbit. The unmanned Soviet Zond 5 probe had already sent two tortoises, flies, and mealworms on a trip around the Moon. The United States wanted the first humans to orbit the Moon to be Americans. It badly wanted to win this space milestone.

NASA moved up its launch schedule. Instead of simply testing equipment in Earth orbit, Apollo 8 would now go all the way to the Moon and back. The mission would test how well spacecraft could navigate between Earth and the Moon. This knowledge would set the stage for later Apollo missions.

EARTHRISE

On Christmas Eve, December 24, 1968, as the Apollo 8 astronauts orbited the Moon, they witnessed a wondrous sight. There was the Earth, rising up over the Moon's horizon. Photographed by Bill Anders, the image has come to be known as "Earthrise." Said Anders, "We came all this way to explore the Moon, and the most important thing is that we discovered the Earth."

21

MISSION: Apollo 8
ROCKET: Saturn V
DATE: December 21-27, 1968
ASTRONAUTS: Frank Borman, Jim Lovell, William Anders

Apollo 8 astronauts (left to right) were Jim Lovell, command module pilot; William Anders, lunar module pilot, and Frank Borman, commander.

Apollo 8's crew included Commander Frank Borman, James Lovell, and William Anders. Borman and Lovell previously flew together on Gemini 7. Lovell had also flown on Gemini 12. Apollo 8 would be William Anders's first trip to space.

On December 21, 1968, Apollo 8's enormous Saturn V rocket rumbled to life and lifted off from Kennedy Space Center's Launch Pad 39A in Florida. It was the first manned flight of a Saturn V, and all systems were go. After reaching Earth orbit, the crew performed a perfect 17-second burn of the rocket's third stage. The rocket fell away, sending Apollo 8 on its three-day trip to the Moon.

On the third day, Apollo 8 slipped around the far side of the Moon. All radio contact with Earth was lost during this time. The crew performed a rocket burn that slowed the spacecraft enough to be captured by the Moon's gravity and place it in orbit. If they had made a mistake, Apollo 8 could have missed its orbit and been hurled into space forever. There was a huge sigh of relief from Mission Control when radio contact resumed, and the crew reported that all was well.

Because they had traveled from Earth with the spacecraft pointed backward, the crew members only now got their first good close-up view of the Moon. Jim Lovell remarked at how gray and colorless the lunar surface appeared. They were all amazed at the number of craters they could see, some of them quite huge.

During 20 hours of orbiting the Moon, the crew took detailed photos of the lunar surface. These images would help pinpoint landing sites for later Apollo missions.

On Christmas Eve, the Apollo 8 crew gave an emotional television address to the people back home on Earth. They described the black void of space, and the desolation of the Moon. Then each man read a part of the Bible's Book of Genesis, about the creation of the Earth. Frank Borman finished the broadcast with these now-famous words: "And from the crew of Apollo 8, we close with good night, good luck, a Merry Christmas and God bless all of you—all of you on the good Earth."

After a three-day return flight, Apollo 8 splashed down safely in the Pacific Ocean on December 27, 1968. Borman, Lovell, and Anders were welcomed home as heroes.

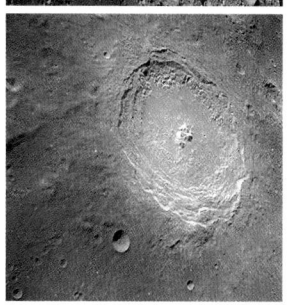

Moon photos from the Apollo 8 mission.

APOLLO 9

MISSION: Apollo 9
ROCKET: Saturn V
DATE: March 3-13, 1969
ASTRONAUTS: James McDivitt, David Scott, Russell Schweickart

Apollo 9 lifted off on March 3, 1969, about two months after Apollo 8's historic flight around the Moon. Astronauts James McDivitt, David Scott, and Russell "Rusty" Schweickart stayed closer to home, limited to orbiting Earth. They tested the lunar module to make sure it was safe for Moon missions. It was the first time the lunar module flew with a crew.

When launched, the lunar module was tucked underneath the command module. After the command module was released in orbit, it turned around and docked with the lunar module, pulling it away from its protective shell. The astronauts named their command module *Gumdrop*. The lunar module was called *Spider* because of its odd shape. During the mission, the astronauts flew *Spider* on its own, and simulated a return from the Moon.

Russell Schweickart, Lunar Module Pilot

David Scott, Command Module Pilot

James McDivitt, Commander

The lunar module *Spider* is tested by astronauts McDivitt and Schweickart while they orbit the Earth.

24

APOLLO 10

MISSION: Apollo 10
ROCKET: Saturn V
DATE: May 18-26, 1969
ASTRONAUTS: Tom Stafford, John Young, Gene Cernan

Apollo 10's mission was to orbit the Moon, just like Apollo 8. However, this time a lunar lander would also be traveling along. Apollo 10 lifted off on May 18, 1969. The mission was a dress rehearsal for Apollo 11, which was scheduled to land on the Moon later that summer. Apollo 10's crew included Thomas Stafford, Gene Cernan, and John Young. They named their command module *Charlie Brown* and the lunar module *Snoopy*.

Gene Cernan, Lunar Module Pilot

Tom Stafford, Commander

John Young, Command Module Pilot

While Young stayed behind and flew *Charlie Brown*, Stafford and Cernan descended in *Snoopy*. They got within nine miles (14 km) of the lunar surface before they turned back. It was a bittersweet moment for the astronauts, to have come so far without landing on the Moon. However, their tests and measurements would be a big help for the historic Moon landing to come.

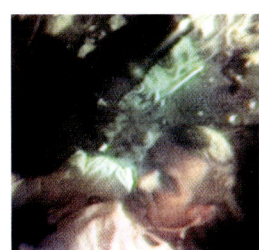

Images of Tom Stafford, John Young (showing Charlie Brown and Snoopy), and Gene Cernan while in space.

APOLLO 11

MISSION: Apollo 11
ROCKET: Saturn V
DATE: July 16-24, 1969
ASTRONAUTS: Neil Armstrong, Buzz Aldrin, Michael Collins

In 1961, President John F. Kennedy challenged the nation to put astronauts on the Moon before the end of the decade. "No single space project," he said, "will be more impressive to mankind, or more important for the long-range exploration of space, and none will be so difficult or expensive to accomplish."

On July 16, 1969, President Kennedy's wish was about to come true. On that day, American astronauts Neil Armstrong, Edwin "Buzz" Aldrin, and Michael Collins began their historic Apollo 11 Moon mission. From Florida's Kennedy Space Center, their Saturn V rocket billowed fire and smoke, launching the crew into Earth orbit. Soon, their command module *Columbia* was docked to the lunar module *Eagle*. All was going according to plan. They were beginning a three-day journey that would take them nearly a quarter million miles (402,336 km) through space to the Moon and a date with history.

Neil Armstrong, Commander

Michael Collins, Command Module Pilot

Buzz Aldrin, Lunar Module Pilot

Apollo 11 lifts off.

The lunar module is photographed by Michael Collins as it descends toward the Moon with astronauts Neil Armstrong and Buzz Aldrin aboard.

On July 20, 1969, Neil Armstrong and Buzz Aldrin descended in the *Eagle* toward a spot on the Moon called the Sea of Tranquility. Millions of people on Earth were glued to their radios and televisions.

As Michael Collins orbited the Moon in *Columbia*, Armstrong and Aldrin rode in the cramped cabin of the lunar module, its four insect-like legs extended and ready to land. Their eyes darted over the panel of glowing buttons and switches in front of them. Word came from Mission Control: "You are go for powered descent."

When they were exactly 50,174 feet (15,293 m) above the Moon and 192 miles (309 km) from the landing site, the astronauts ignited the engine beneath them. Their speed decreased, and the Moon's gravity began pulling them toward the surface.

Eagle's computer guided them down. Armstrong and Aldrin felt the lunar module shake as control thrusters fired automatically to keep them on course.

A shrill alarm sounded in the cabin. *Eagle's* main computer had become overloaded with information. The astronauts prepared to abort the mission. Mission Control decided *Eagle's* computer was still working properly. The mission continued.

When they were 1,300 feet (396 m) above the surface, Armstrong looked out the window and saw they had overshot the landing site. The ground was strewn with boulders. Armstrong took over manual control of *Eagle*. Using all his skills as an astronaut and pilot, he expertly guided *Eagle* to a safer area. Their fuel level was critically low. They were in real danger of crashing.

Finally, after long moments of silence, Mission Control heard Armstrong on the radio, his voice calm and professional: "Houston, Tranquility Base here. The *Eagle* has landed."

Buzz Aldrin steps down from the *Eagle*.

Buzz Aldrin stands by the American flag he and Neil Armstrong planted on the Moon.

About four hours after landing on the Moon, Neil Armstrong swung open *Eagle's* hatch. He saw before him a barren, windless lunar landscape under a black sky.

Armstrong stepped from the lunar module's cabin onto a ladder. He carefully stepped down each rung, toward a world no human, or any living thing, had ever visited. A TV camera on the side of the lunar lander broadcast Armstrong as he reached the last step.

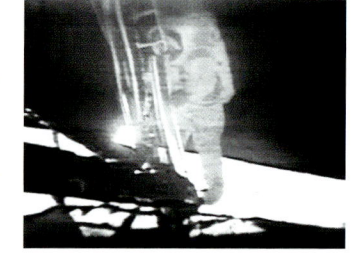

Armstrong's first step on the Moon was broadcast to millions of people on Earth.

More than 500 million people on Earth watched as Armstrong seemed to float down to the disk-shaped foot at the end of the lander's leg. (The Moon has just one-sixth the gravity of Earth.) Then, he pressed his left foot carefully into the lunar soil, leaving behind a perfect bootprint. Armstrong spoke into his spacesuit radio. "That's one small step for a man, one giant leap for mankind."

About 20 minutes later, Buzz Aldrin joined Armstrong on the Moon's surface. Before starting their long list of tasks and experiments, the two astronauts took a moment to view the scene around them. "It has a very stark beauty all its own," Armstrong said of the crater-pocked surface. A fine gray powder—Moon dust—covered almost everything.

Buzz Aldrin felt awed by the Moon's gray and tan colors, and the sharp shadows cast by the Sun. "Beautiful, beautiful!" he exclaimed. "Magnificent desolation."

After spending 21 hours on the Moon, Armstrong and Aldrin reunited with Michael Collins in *Columbia* and began the three-day journey home. They brought back about 49 pounds (22 kg) of Moon rocks. They left science experiments, unneeded equipment, an American flag, and a plaque that read, "Here men from the planet Earth first set foot upon the Moon, July 1969 A.D. We came in peace for all mankind."

With the successful landing on Earth of Apollo 11 on July 24, 1969, America won the Space Race with the Soviet Union. But there were many missions yet to come, and much more to be explored.

PRESIDENTIAL THANK YOU

On July 24, 1969, Apollo 11 astronauts Armstrong, Collins, and Aldrin (left to right) are visited by President Richard M. Nixon aboard the recovery ship USS *Hornet*. The astronauts were in quarantine, kept away from others in case they had picked up any unknown space germs. They received thanks from Americans and people around the world.

APOLLO 12

MISSION: Apollo 12
ROCKET: Saturn V
DATE: November 14-24, 1969
ASTRONAUTS: Pete Conrad, Richard Gordon, Alan Bean

Just four months after Apollo 11's historic mission, Apollo 12 lifted off from Florida's Kennedy Space Center on November 14, 1969. The mission started with some bad luck. As the Saturn V rocket passed through a storm cloud, it was struck by lightning. The spacecraft's electrical systems were knocked out, but backup power quickly came on. All systems were reset, and Apollo 12 was ready to continue.

In three days, astronauts Charles "Pete" Conrad, Alan Bean, and Richard Gordon reached the Moon, nearly a quarter million miles (402,336 km) from Earth.

Charles "Pete" Conrad, Commander

Richard Gordon, Command Module Pilot

Alan Bean, Lunar Module Pilot

A rare photo of two United States spacecraft on the Moon. Astronaut Pete Conrad examines Surveyor 3, with the *Intrepid* in the background.

As Gordon piloted the command module *Yankee Clipper*, Conrad and Bean descended to the Moon in the lunar module *Intrepid*. They made a pinpoint landing on the Moon's Ocean of Storms region. (Conrad nicknamed their landing site "Pete's Parking Lot.") After landing, the astronauts were excited to walk on the Moon. "Those rocks have been waiting four and a half billion years for us to come grab them," said Bean. "Let's go grab a few."

The astronauts performed a pair of four-hour moonwalks, or extravehicular activities (EVAs). They collected rock samples, set up science experiments, and measured the Moon's magnetic field. They also took a short hike to Surveyor 3. It was an American lunar lander that touched down on the Moon two years earlier, in 1967. Conrad and Bean took several parts of Surveyor 3 back with them to Earth.

APOLLO 13

MISSION: Apollo 13
ROCKET: Saturn V
DATE: April 11-17, 1970
ASTRONAUTS: Jim Lovell, Jack Swigert, Fred Haise

Apollo 13 lifted off from Florida's Kennedy Space Center on April 11, 1970. The three astronauts aboard included James Lovell, Fred Haise, and John "Jack" Swigert. Originally, the crew included astronaut Ken Mattingly. However, he was exposed to German measles and was replaced by Swigert three days before launch.

Jim Lovell, Commander   Jack Swigert, Command Module Pilot   Fred Haise, Lunar Module Pilot

Lovell, the commander, was a veteran astronaut who also flew on Gemini 7, Gemini 12, and Apollo 8. Apollo 13 was his chance to finally walk on the Moon.

All seemed to be going well as they sped toward the Moon, nestled safely inside the command module *Odyssey*. Then, almost 56 hours into the mission, the crew heard a bang and felt the spacecraft shake.

"HOUSTON, WE'VE HAD A PROBLEM."

Apollo 13's famous words, "Houston, we've had a problem," were said by Jack Swigert and repeated by commander Jim Lovell to Mission Control on April 13, 1970. A photo of the badly damaged service module was taken from the command module *Odyssey*.

34

The Apollo 13 astronauts got little sleep in their freezing spacecraft.

The astronauts could only look at the Moon as they passed by. Their new mission was to get home.

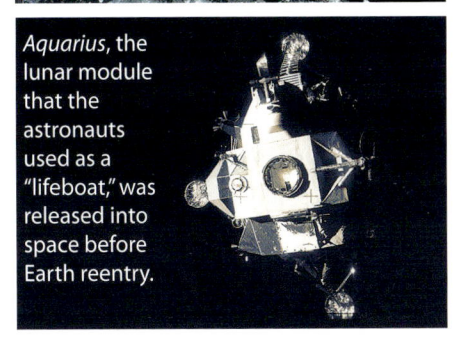

Aquarius, the lunar module that the astronauts used as a "lifeboat," was released into space before Earth reentry.

The world cheered as the astronauts returned safe.

Damaged wires had sparked a fire inside an oxygen tank in the service module. The tank blew up with the force of a shotgun blast, damaging wiring, pipes, and valves. One side of the service module was blown outward.

Lovell could see a cloud of gas venting into space from the side of the crippled spacecraft. He knew they were in deep trouble. The explosion knocked out most of the command module's electricity, water, and heat. To make matters worse, they were more than 200,000 miles (321,869 km) from Earth.

The crew moved into the lunar module *Aquarius* and used it as a lifeboat. With the help of scientists at Mission Control, they were able to slingshot around the Moon and head back home. The astronauts suffered for several days with little to drink or eat, with almost no sleep, and freezing cold temperatures. At last, they reached Earth. They moved back into *Odyssey*, and on April 17, 1970, safely splashed down in the Pacific Ocean.

APOLLO 14

MISSION: Apollo 14
ROCKET: Saturn V
DATE: Jan. 31-Feb. 9, 1971
ASTRONAUTS: Alan Shepard, Edgar Mitchell, Stuart Roosa

After the Apollo 13 disaster, several changes were made to the service module. The oxygen tanks were redesigned to prevent the kind of explosion that crippled the spacecraft. Also, a third tank was added, just in case.

After a four-month delay, Apollo 14 lifted into the sky like crackling thunder on January 31, 1971. Riding atop the Saturn V rocket were astronauts Alan Shepard, the commander of the mission, plus Stuart Roosa and Edgar Mitchell. For Shepard, this flight was a long-awaited comeback. He was one of the original Mercury 7 astronauts, and the first American to fly in space. Medical conditions had kept him grounded for several years, but now he was cleared to fly in space again. With the Apollo 14 mission, Alan Shepard would become the only Mercury 7 astronaut to walk on the Moon.

Alan Shepard, Commander

Edgar Mitchell, Lunar Module Pilot

Stuart Roosa, Command Module Pilot

Alan Shepard conducts an experiment on the Moon with the mission's scientific laboratory.

The command module on this mission was named *Kitty Hawk*. It would be flown solo by Stuart Roosa during the Moon landing. The lunar module was named *Antares*.

On February 5, 1971, *Antares* began its decent to the Moon with astronauts Shepard and Mitchell inside. A computer glitch and a radar malfunction almost caused the mission to abort, but quick thinking by Mission Control and the astronauts saved the day. Shepard put *Antares* down closer to the landing zone than any other Apollo mission.

Shepard and Mitchell went on two moonwalks totaling more than nine hours. The pair collected 94 pounds (43 kg) of rocks, and conducted several science experiments. Shepard even hit two golf balls with a club he'd brought with him. In the Moon's low gravity, Shepard said the second ball went "Miles and miles and miles."

Alan Shepard hits a golf ball on the Moon.

The crew of Apollo 14 returned to Earth on February 9, 1971, splashing down safely in the Pacific Ocean.

APOLLO 15

MISSION: Apollo 15
ROCKET: Saturn V
DATE: July 26–August 7, 1971
ASTRONAUTS: David Scott, James Irwin, Alfred Worden

On the morning of July 26, 1971, Apollo 15 lifted off from the Kennedy Space Center in Florida. The mission included astronauts David Scott, James Irwin, and Al Worden. Soon, they were on their way to the Moon. The command module on this mission was named *Endeavor*. The lunar module was called *Falcon*.

David Scott, Commander   Alfred Worden, Command Module Pilot   James Irwin, Lunar Module Pilot

On July 30, after orbiting the Moon several times, Commander Scott and lunar module pilot Irwin began their descent in *Falcon*. Command module pilot Worden flew solo in *Endeavor* while taking high-resolution photos of the Moon's surface below.

Falcon landed on the foothills of the Moon's Montes Appenninus region (named after the Apennine Mountains in Italy). The mountains rose an average of 15,000 feet (4,572 m) above the lunar plain, about the height of Colorado's Mount Evans.

David Scott was the first driver on the Moon.

LUNAR ROVING VEHICLE (LRV)

The electric-powered LRV weighed only 460 pounds (209 kg), but could carry up to 1,500 pounds (680 kg), including two astronauts. It reached speeds of 6-8 miles per hour (10-13 kph).

Over three days, during three moonwalks totaling 18.5 hours, Scott and Irwin collected Moon rocks and performed many science experiments. They also used a new piece of equipment: the lunar roving vehicle (LRV), a battery-powered cart that traveled about 8 miles per hour (13 kph). It brought the astronauts to distant landmarks and carried heavy loads of rocks and equipment. Using the rover, the astronauts traveled 17.5 miles (28 km), breaking Apollo 14's record of 2.1 miles (3.4 km).

During the trip back to Earth, Al Worden performed the first spacewalk in deep space. He was sent outside the capsule to retrieve film for a science experiment attached to the spacecraft's hull. *Endeavor* safely splashed down in the Pacific Ocean on August 7, 1971.

Astronaut James Irwin salutes the United States flag at the *Falcon* landing site in the foothills of the Moon's Montes Appenninus region.

APOLLO 16

MISSION: Apollo 16
ROCKET: Saturn V
DATE: April 16-27, 1972
ASTRONAUTS: John Young, Ken Mattingly, Charles Duke

On April 19, 1972, Apollo 16's command module *Casper* slipped into orbit around the Moon. The next day, Commander John Young and astronaut Charles Duke climbed into the lunar module *Orion* and undocked. Astronaut Ken Mattingly stayed behind and flew *Casper* solo as his crewmates began their descent to the Moon.

Ken Mattingly, Command Module Pilot

John Young, Commander

Charles Duke, Lunar Module Pilot

Orion landed in the Descartes Highlands region. It was the first Apollo mission in that part of the Moon. NASA wanted to sample rocks from the area. Geologists were interested to see if there were differences from samples retrieved by earlier missions.

Astronaut John Young gives the lunar roving vehicle a speed workout at the Descartes Highlands landing site.

"YOU DO THAT IN WEST TEXAS AND YOU GET A RATTLESNAKE!"

When John Young reached under a boulder to collect soil, Charles Duke said that the commander would have a surprise waiting if he did that in Texas.

Young and Duke spent a total of 71 hours on the lunar surface. They took three moonwalks totaling about 20 hours. During that time, they collected 209 pounds (95 kg) of rock samples. They drove their rover almost 17 miles (27 km) across the gray lunar landscape.

In addition to collecting rock, Young and Duke conducted science experiments, including measuring the Moon's magnetic field. They also explored several deep craters and took hundreds of photographs.

On April 24, Young and Duke loaded their rock samples into *Orion*. They strapped themselves in and lifted off in the lunar module's ascent stage. Once in orbit, they docked with *Casper* and transferred their equipment to the command module. Next, they prepared for the journey back to Earth.

On April 27, 1972, the astronauts safely splashed down in the Pacific Ocean. They were picked up by rescue crews from the Navy aircraft carrier USS *Ticonderoga* about a half-hour after splashdown.

APOLLO 17

MISSION: Apollo 17
ROCKET: Saturn V
DATE: December 7-19, 1972
ASTRONAUTS: Gene Cernan, Harrison Schmitt, Ronald Evans

Apollo 17 was the last flight of NASA's Apollo missions. Riding inside the command module *America* were astronauts Gene Cernan, Ronald Evans, and Harrison Schmitt. Their Saturn V rocket lifted off on the night of December 7, 1972. When the Saturn V's engines ignited, an orange fireball lit up the sky as Apollo 17 sped away from Earth.

On December 11, Cernan and Schmitt descended to the Moon in the lunar module *Challenger*. After a smooth landing on the Moon's Taurus-Littrow region, Cernan and Schmitt went on three moonwalks over three days. They collected 243 pounds (110 kg) of rock samples. They also took photographs of the area, performed science experiments, and explored the boulder-strewn landscape.

Harrison Schmitt, Lunar Module Pilot   Gene Cernan, Commander   Ronald Evans, Command Module Pilot

BIG BOULDERS

Harrison Schmitt shows the size of one of the Moon's boulders near the Apollo 17 landing site. The lunar rover is parked nearby.

Finally, it was time to go home. Commander Gene Cernan was the last Apollo astronaut to leave the Moon. Before he entered *Challenger*, he took one last look at the desolate, beautiful, alien world. He radioed Mission Control, saying, "As I take man's last step from the surface… for some time to come—but we believe not too long into the future—I'd like to just say what I believe history will record. That America's challenge of today has forged man's destiny of tomorrow. And, as we leave the Moon at Taurus-Littrow, we leave as we came and, God willing, as we shall return, with peace and hope for all mankind. Godspeed the crew of Apollo 17."

Cernan, Evans, and Schmitt splashed down in the *America* in the Pacific Ocean on December 19, 1972. Project Apollo had come to a spectacular end.

TIMELINE

1957, October 4—The Soviet Union launches the Sputnik 1 satellite. It marks the unofficial start of the Space Race.

1958, October 1—National Aeronautics and Space Administration (NASA), a United States government agency, officially begins work. It is a civilian agency, separate from the military, that coordinates and carries out America's space activities, both manned and unmanned.

1961-1963—NASA's Project Mercury completes 6 successful missions, including America's first man in space and the first orbits of the Earth.

1964-1966—NASA's Project Gemini completes 12 successful missions, including the first American spacewalk, docking, and multiday missions.

1967, January 27—Apollo 1 astronauts Gus Grissom, Ed White, and Roger Chaffee are killed in a fire in the capsule while training. Their deaths will result in new safety standards for future manned missions.

1967-1968—Unmanned test flights for Apollo 4, 5, and 6. (There was no Apollo 2 or 3.)

1968, October 11-22—Apollo 7 astronauts Wally Schirra, Walt Cunningham, and Donn Eisele fly the first manned mission since the Apollo 1 tragedy. They test the command and service modules.

1968, December 21-27—Apollo 8 astronauts Frank Borman, Jim Lovell, and William Anders orbit the Moon and take the first "Earthrise" photo.

1969, March 3-13—Apollo 9 astronauts James McDivitt, David Scott, and Russell Schweickart test the lunar module while orbiting Earth.

1969, May 18-26—Apollo 10 astronauts Tom Stafford, John Young, and Gene Cernan travel to the Moon and descend partway in the lunar module.

1969, July 16-24—Apollo 11 astronauts Neil Armstrong, Buzz Aldrin, and Michael Collins travel to the Moon. On July 20, Armstrong and Aldrin descend to the lunar surface. Armstrong's words become famous as he becomes the first man to step on the Moon: "That's one small step for a man, one giant leap for mankind."

1969, November 14-24—Apollo 12 astronauts Pete Conrad, Richard Gordon, and Alan Bean travel to the Moon. Conrad and Bean descend to the lunar surface. They collect rocks and conduct experiments.

1970, April 11-17—Apollo 13 astronauts Jim Lovell, Jack Swigert, and Fred Haise, two days into their mission, have an explosion that cripples their service module and puts them in extreme danger. The world listens and watches until the astronauts return safely to Earth.

1971, Jan. 31-Feb. 9—Apollo 14 astronauts Alan Shepard, Stuart Roosa, and Edgar Mitchell travel to the Moon. Shepard and Mitchell go down to the surface for EVAs. Shepard hits two golf balls.

1971, July 26-Aug. 7—Apollo 15 astronauts David Scott, James Irwin, and Al Worden travel to the Moon. First lunar roving vehicle is driven.

1972, April 16-27—Apollo 16 astronauts John Young, Ken Mattingly, and Charles Duke travel to the Moon. Young gives the rover a speed test.

1972, December 7-19—Apollo 17 astronauts Gene Cernan, Harrison Schmitt, and Ronald Evans travel to the Moon. They conduct experiments and collect samples. Gene Cernan becomes the last man to walk on the Moon. Their mission ends Project Apollo.

GLOSSARY

Astronaut
Someone who travels in a spacecraft. The word has Greek roots that stand for "star sailor" or "star traveller."

Cosmonaut
An astronaut from Russia or the former Soviet Union.

Diameter
The distance through the center of an object, from one side to the other.

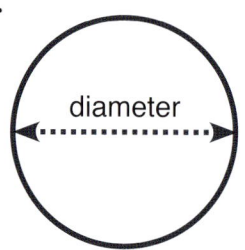

Dock
When either two spacecraft or a spacecraft and a space station are joined together.

Extravehicular Activity (EVA)
An EVA is any activity for which astronauts must go outside the protected environment in which they live while in space. A moonwalk is an EVA.

National Aeronautics and Space Administration (NASA)
A United States government space agency started in 1958. NASA's goals include space exploration and increasing people's understanding of Earth, our solar system, and the universe.

Orbit
The path a moon or spacecraft makes when traveling around a planet or other large celestial body.

Rendezvous
A meeting at a specific time and place.

Sea of Tranquility
Apollo 11's Neil Armstrong and Buzz Aldrin landed in the Sea of Tranquility. It is a large region of the Moon made mostly of basalt rock. Early astronomers once thought the dark areas of the Moon were filled with water. That is why they are named for seas. In reality, they are dark because the rocks are rich in iron, which reflects less light.

Soviet Union
A former country that included a union of Russia and several other Communist republics. It was formed in 1922 and existed until 1991.

Splashdown
When Apollo spacecraft returned to Earth, they landed in the ocean—thus, a splashdown.

Stage
In order to fly as high as possible, some rockets have more than one section, called stages. Each stage has its own engine and fuel. They are stacked on top of each other. When the first stage runs out of fuel, it drops away and falls toward Earth.

ONLINE RESOURCES

Booklinks NONFICTION NETWORK
FREE! ONLINE NONFICTION RESOURCES

To learn more about Project Apollo, visit **abdobooklinks.com** or scan this QR code. These links are routinely monitored and updated to provide the most current information available.

INDEX

A
Aldrin, Edwin "Buzz" 4, 26, 28, 31
America (*see also* Apollo 17) 42, 43
America (*see* United States)
Anders, William 22, 23
Antares 37
Apennine Mountains 38
Apollo 1 14, 16
Apollo 4 18
Apollo 5 18
Apollo 6 18
Apollo 7 12, 18, 19, 20
Apollo 8 20, 22, 23, 24, 25, 34
Apollo 9 24
Apollo 10 25
Apollo 11 6, 12, 25, 26, 31, 32
Apollo 12 32
Apollo 13 34, 36
Apollo 14 36, 37, 39
Apollo 15 38
Apollo 16 40
Apollo 17 12, 42, 43
Aquarius 35
Armstrong, Neil 4, 26, 28, 29, 30, 31
Atlantic Ocean 19

B
Baikonur Cosmodrome 16
Bean, Alan 32, 33
Bible 23
Book of Genesis 23
Borman, Frank 22, 23
Brezhnev, Leonid 16

C
Cape Canaveral 18
Casper 40, 41
Cernan, Gene 25, 42, 43
Chaffee, Roger 14
Challenger 42, 43
Charlie Brown 25
Collins, Michael 26, 28, 31
Colorado 38
Columbia 26, 28, 31
command module 10, 11, 14, 18, 19, 24, 25, 26, 33, 34, 37, 38, 40, 42
Conrad, Charles "Pete" 32, 33
Cunningham, Walt 18

D
Descartes Highlands 40
Duke, Charles 40, 41

E
Eagle 26, 28, 29, 30
Earth 4, 6, 7, 10, 12, 17, 19, 20, 22, 23, 24, 26, 28, 30, 31, 32, 33, 35, 37, 39, 41, 42
Eisele, Donn 18
Endeavor 38, 39
Evans, Mount 38
Evans, Ronald 42, 43

F
Falcon 38
Florida 18, 22, 26, 32, 34, 38

G
Gemini 4 14
Gemini 7 22, 34
Gemini 12 22, 34
Gemini, Project 4, 10, 14, 16, 19
Gordon, Richard 32, 33
Grissom, Virgil "Gus" 14
Gumdrop 24

H
Haise, Fred 34
Houston, TX 19, 29

I
Intrepid 33
Irwin, James 38, 39
Italy 38

K
Kazakhstan, Soviet Union 16
Kennedy, John F. 26
Kennedy Space Center 22, 26, 32, 34, 38
Kitty Hawk 37
Komarov, Vladimir 16, 17
Korolev, Sergei 9

L
Launch Pad 39A 22
Liberty Bell 7 14
Lovell, James "Jim" 22, 23, 34, 35
Luna 2 6, 7
Luna 3 7
Luna 9 7
lunar module 11, 12, 18, 24, 25, 26, 28, 30, 33, 35, 37, 38, 40, 41, 42
lunar roving vehicle (LRV) 39

M
Mattingly, Ken 34, 40
McDivitt, James 24
Mercury 7 36
Mercury, Project 4, 10, 14, 19
Mission Control 19, 22, 28, 29, 35, 37, 43
Mitchell, Edgar 36, 37
monster rockets (*see* Saturn V) 8
Montes Appenninus 38
Moon 4, 6, 7, 8, 9, 10, 11, 12, 16, 17, 19, 20, 22, 23, 24, 25, 26, 28, 30, 31, 32, 33, 34, 35, 36, 37, 38, 39, 40, 41, 42, 43

N
N-1 Rocket 9
NASA 6, 7, 12, 16, 20, 40, 42
National Aeronautics and Space Administration (*see* NASA) 6
Navy, U.S. 14, 41

O
Ocean of Storms 33
Odyssey 34, 35
Orion 40, 41

P
Pacific Ocean 23, 35, 37, 39, 41, 43
Pete's Parking Lot 33
Pioneer 4 7

R
Ranger 7 7
Ranger 8 7
Ranger 9 7
Roosa, Stuart 36, 37
Russia 4

S
Saturn 1B 14, 18
Saturn V 8, 9, 18, 22, 24, 25, 26, 32, 34, 36, 38, 40, 42
Schirra, Wally 18, 19
Schmitt, Harrison 42, 43
Schweickart, Russell "Rusty" 24
Scott, David 24, 38, 39
Sea of Tranquility 28
service module 11
Shepard, Alan 36, 37
Snoopy 25
Soviet Union 4, 6, 7, 9, 16, 17, 20, 31
Soyuz 16
Soyuz 1 16, 17
Soyuz 2 17
Soyuz 11 17
Spider 24
Stafford, Thomas "Tom" 25
Statue of Liberty 8
Sun 31
Surveyor 1 7
Surveyor 3 33
Swigert, John "Jack" 34

T
Taurus-Littrow 42, 43
Texas 19
Ticonderoga, USS 41
Tranquility Base 29

U
United States 4, 6, 7, 8, 9, 17, 20, 31, 43

V
von Braun, Wernher 8

W
White, Edward "Ed" 14
Worden, Alfred "Al" 38
World War II 8

Y
Yankee Clipper 33
Young, John 25, 40, 41

Z
Zond 5 probe 20

48